Slowpoke Snail

written by Y. Kimchi
illustrated by Carlos Ochagavia

HARCOURT BRACE & COMPANY

Orlando   Atlanta   Austin   Boston   San Francisco   Chicago   Dallas   New York
Toronto   London

Frogs and fish move fast. Most birds and bees do, too. But the little snail does not move fast. Why IS a snail so slow?

A hungry bird lands close by. He thinks he's found a fine meal. But the snail takes his time. He tucks in his head and slowly moves away.

A hungry fish swims close by. He thinks he's found a fine meal. But the snail takes his time. He tucks in his foot and slowly moves away.

If a bird or a fish wants to eat him, the snail is not afraid. He just goes inside and hides.

Now you know why a snail is so slow. He doesn't have to be fast!